ISNESS

WHEN ONLY THE SILENCE REMAINS

PATRICIA GRAY

FriesenPress

One Printers Way
Altona, MB R0G 0B0
Canada

www.friesenpress.com

Copyright © 2025 by Patricia Gray MA
First Edition — 2025

All illustrations are original paintings done by the author.

Front cover illustration: *A Morning Meditation*

Author photo by Theresa Gray

All rights reserved.

No part of this publication may be reproduced in any form, or by any means, electronic or mechanical, including photocopying, recording, or any information browsing, storage, or retrieval system, without permission in writing from FriesenPress.

ISBN
978-1-03-832289-0 (Hardcover)
978-1-03-832288-3 (Paperback)
978-1-03-832290-6 (eBook)

1. BODY, MIND & SPIRIT, MYSTICISM

Distributed to the trade by The Ingram Book Company

DISCLAIMER

No part of this book is intended to be a substitute for in-person, or one-on-one professional psychological, psychiatric, or medical counselling, treatment or diagnosis. Never disregard professional psychological, psychiatric, or medical advice or delay in seeking it if you are experiencing any issues or concerns regarding your mental, emotional, or physical health.

This book is not meant to be utilized in whole or in part as a psychotherapeutic tool (except at the informed discretion of a qualified mental health practitioner whose scope of practice includes non-dual psychotherapy) or intervention or as a substitute and/or replacement for psychological, psychiatric, or medical treatment or advice.

This book does not in any way constitute a client–therapist relationship. Patricia Gray will not be liable for claims or damages and expressly disclaims any and all liability of any nature, for any action taken or not taken as a result of reading this book.

For Jaimi and Gray
You are manifestations of love, beauty, and grace.
My joy and inspiration.

And for Mark
Waadosemid.
Still "honouring the Mystery"…

Deep gratitude to Sri Ramana Maharshi and Sri Nisargadatta Maharaj for illuminating the Way.

And to Hans Laurentius
I am ever grateful for our "chance" encounter on the way Home.

Gichi-miigwech

Mitchell Akerman for the Anishinaabemowin teachings and for continuing to breathe life into the language and culture.

Cheri Richman for falling into my world and your readiness to lend a hand all the way from New Jersey.

Donna Evans for your ongoing friendship, encouragement and unwavering support from the opposite side of the world.

Lorraine Ross for "finding" me in childhood and the decades of friendship and love. Donna Glenesk for all the times we have shared along the "Mighty Moose River," and for managing to capture its Spirit in the photograph that I have included in this book. And to her "forever partner," Tony Turner, my good friend and wilderness guide, for helping to make our northern adventures so memorable and keeping us safe by being able to "read" the river so skillfully.

Jeanie Fountain for your friendship, support and palpable enthusiasm.

And to my "Sis," for capturing such a beautiful "back cover moment" on the stunning waters of Georgian Bay.

A NOTE ON HOW TO BEST APPROACH THIS BOOK...

This book of reflections, or "pointings," is intended to *speak to* that which lies beyond the intellect. And so, to intuit the deeper meanings and subtle nuances behind them, they will need to be contemplated within the *quietness of your heart*. Simply pausing and bringing your full attention to whatever resonates with you will create a space for the words to merge with your *being*, naturally and effortlessly. *Don't overthink!*

PREFACE

As a child, I had a profound *inner knowing* that I was not who I *appeared* to be—that the way I was being perceived by those around me was somehow foreign and inconsequential to "what" I truly was.

On an intuitive level, I understood a deeper truth: that I was intimately connected to and an integral part of, something much bigger than "me." Something deeply *mysterious,* yet beautifully *familiar*. Of course, as a young child this understanding was not in any way conceptual, yet a deeper reality was intuited. And it was a tremendous source of sustenance.

This *knowing* remained with me. And many years later, although at the time I did not understand what it was, I had a spontaneous *glimpse* into the *Isness*, into the *pure essence of Being*. While I was driving and just minding my own business!, there was the sudden recognition that there was simply "no one" there. No "experiencer." Driving was simply *taking place*. I could see everything along my route but there was no one *doing* the looking. Seeing was simply *happening*. There was no separation, no sense of a "me" *in here* and a world *out there*. Just one seamless, timeless reality. A vast silence in which the *emptiness* of everything was *seen*.

Up to that point in my life I had not heard of *Advaita* or *non-duality*; consequently, I had no idea what had happened, let alone the vocabulary to describe it. I was left truly mystified. But this experience further deepened my interest in Eastern philosophy and spirituality. And eventually, through what I have come to understand as a form of Grace, I came across the teachings of Sri Ramana Maharshi and Sri Nisargadatta Maharaj. Still, it was not until many years later that the existence of a *separate self* was finally revealed as completely illusory. And only then did I recognize that the rather fleeting experience I had all those years before, had been a *piercing through* the *Veil of Maya* – a brief *glimpse* into the unfathomable *Mystery*.

INTRODUCTION

This book is simply an invitation for anyone with a desire to discover or delve deeper into the fundamental nature of their own existence. To find out what they truly are beyond name and form — beyond the person they have been conditioned to believe themselves to be. To no longer identify with the ever-changing workings of their mind, various roles in life, or even their culture, but rather to establish themselves within the stillness of an abiding *Presence* through the direct insight that they already are the peace that they have been longing for. To recognize beyond all doubt that their most fundamental nature is that of *Pure Consciousness.*

I have tried to minimize the use of spiritual language throughout this book because it is becoming increasingly important to find the vocabulary to discuss *Consciousness* and the *nature of reality* that is not necessarily borrowed from the spiritual traditions of the world, especially at this juncture when the conversation is beginning to take its rightful place within the secular realm. We have entered a very exciting time in that science is not only beginning to evolve past the inadequate materialistic view of the world, but also recognize that there is something that exists *beyond* the model of the mathematical structure of *spacetime* that can better explain the universe and reality. Science is finally coming to understand what the mystics have known for thousands of years: it is the primacy of Consciousness, not matter, that is the basis of everything in the universe. And as this paradigm becomes more widely embraced within the scientific community, an increasing number of physicists and neuroscientists are recognizing that the primacy of Consciousness must be the premise upon which all studies related to the *field of Consciousness* are based.

Non-duality, or *Advaita*, from the ancient Sanskrit language, simply means "not two." At its core is the concept that *All is One*: that there are no separate entities but simply one indivisible, infinite reality. That there is *no self*. It is neither a philosophy nor a religion. It has no dogma. It offers no path to follow or beliefs to abide by. It can only be known directly. It suggests that time and space are not *fundamentally real*. That only *emptiness* exists. And although this emptiness is perhaps best described as unconditional or all-encompassing love, it remains beyond every description.

It is important to remember that anything we attempt to communicate about non-duality cannot truly describe it because we must rely on words, concepts, and ideas that are inherently dualistic themselves. And yet, *the Mystery* being what it is, and for no reason at all, appears to compel some of us to try! But doing so requires that we not only acquiesce to the limitations of language, but also become comfortable with the inevitable paradoxes that will arise as we make attempts to ascribe words to the *Ineffable*. To that which transcends not only words but even *thought* itself. In other words, we forge ahead knowing that all we can do is "point" to the Truth, and at times awkwardly at that, all the while knowing that anything that we can say, or even *think* about *It*, cannot be *It*.

For these reasons, this book contains not only several *apparent* contradictions, which when properly grasped will be understood as the aforementioned paradoxes, but also the deliberate repetition of certain ideas and concepts – all in an attempt to convey the truth of "what Is," as clearly and simply as possible.

Liberation, or the *final Understanding*, as it is often referred to, is completely *impersonal*, simply a movement within Consciousness. It has absolutely nothing to do with comprehension, existing beyond anything that we can *imagine* or grasp with our minds. Of course, this can feel like an affront to the ego — to the person we believe ourselves to be — because unlike other things in our lives, we cannot approach these fundamental insights through effort. In fact, the very act of *making an effort* reinforces the belief that there *is* someone *to* make an effort, reinforcing the belief in duality and thus becoming an obstacle in and of itself. Be assured however, that separation never existed in the first place. You are already the *wholeness* that you seek. There is only *This. Infinite, unbounded Awareness*. Once this is *Seen*, it cannot be *unseen*.

Sometimes we must know *the darkness* before we can recognize *our light*. Our suffering may become so intense and our desire for *freedom* so strong, that we will allow nothing to keep us from discovering what we truly are beyond our name and form. The intensity of this yearning can set our *heart on fire for the Truth*, and this fire will burn away everything that we are not… until in the end, *only the silence remains*.

Now, buckle up…!

ISNESS

**Set your life on fire.
Seek those who fan your flames.**

Jalaluddin Rumi

Cast everything aside. Hold onto nothing. Not even a single thought. Abandon all effort. And discover your true nature as *spaceless space. Unbounded.*

THE SEEKER

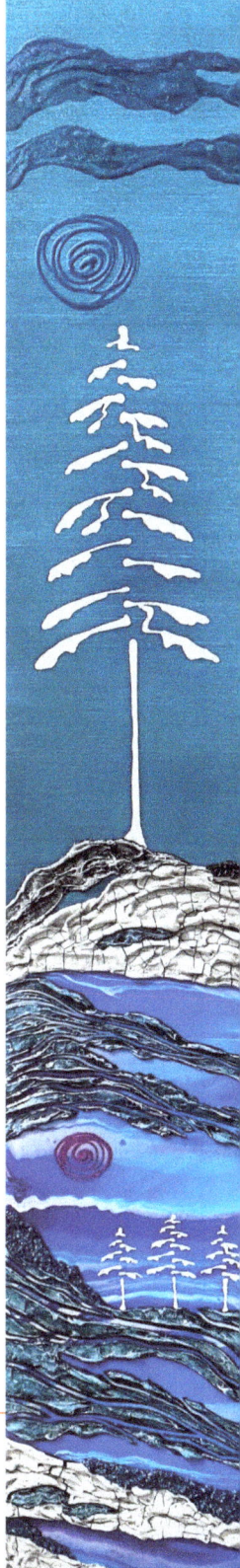

The Truth cannot be spoken. It is beyond the intellect. *Indescribable*. *Ineffable*. Anything we can convey with words cannot be *It*. ❧

Only the *Wordless Truth* — that which exists beyond all thoughts, concepts, and ideas — is *real*.

Leave mind alone. Forget everything you have learned. Your intellect cannot help you here. It will only lead you in circles. Like a dog chasing its own tail, you will be unable to recognize that what you are pursuing, is what you *Are*.

Why embark on such a long and exhausting search to find that which is right here *already*? Somewhere along the way you may have been convinced that if you are just quiet enough, focused enough, disciplined enough, or "spiritual" enough, you just might find *It*.

But *It* has never been lost. You have never been apart from *It*.

You are wandering around looking for our own *Self*.

It is no wonder that the instant of *direct Seeing* is so often met by the spontaneous arising of seemingly inexplicable laughter!

Don't remain in servitude to the mind. What led you to embark on this path of fruitless wandering cannot lead you *Home*.

Nothing obscures the Truth like a *fact*.

The entire world exists within you.
Because of you!

But you cannot imagine *This*!
It is beyond all imaginings.
Beyond all understanding.

In light of this Truth, how could bondage arise?
Rejoice! You are *Freedom Itself*.

JOY!

For the one who seeks the Truth with sincerity,
a natural fervor arises,
and their whole life is instantaneously transformed.
Nothing remains untouched.

The Path is revealed moment to moment.
Pay attention!

Don't allow the *light of your own Being* to be eclipsed by fear. Trust in those who have walked the Path before you to illuminate your way. In times of doubt and uncertainty allow *them* to be your surety.

Be steadfast in your search for Truth.
Trust that it is right *here*.
Right now.

A sincere teacher endeavours to function merely as an intermediator, unceasingly pointing you directly back to the *Sadguru*, or *Inner Teacher*. To the *silence* that has always been within you. That *is* you.

It has never been anything other than *You*.

It is hiding in plain sight.

Let go of all thoughts of "you," even if just for
a moment.
All preoccupations and concerns,
All your perceived successes and failures,
All musings about the past and the future – even your
thoughts and beliefs
about the present moment.

Allow yourself to rest in the quiet stillness of your own
beautiful heart.
In just one moment you can touch all of *Eternity*.

Mind can no more understand the apparent movement of life any more than a river can know where it is flowing.

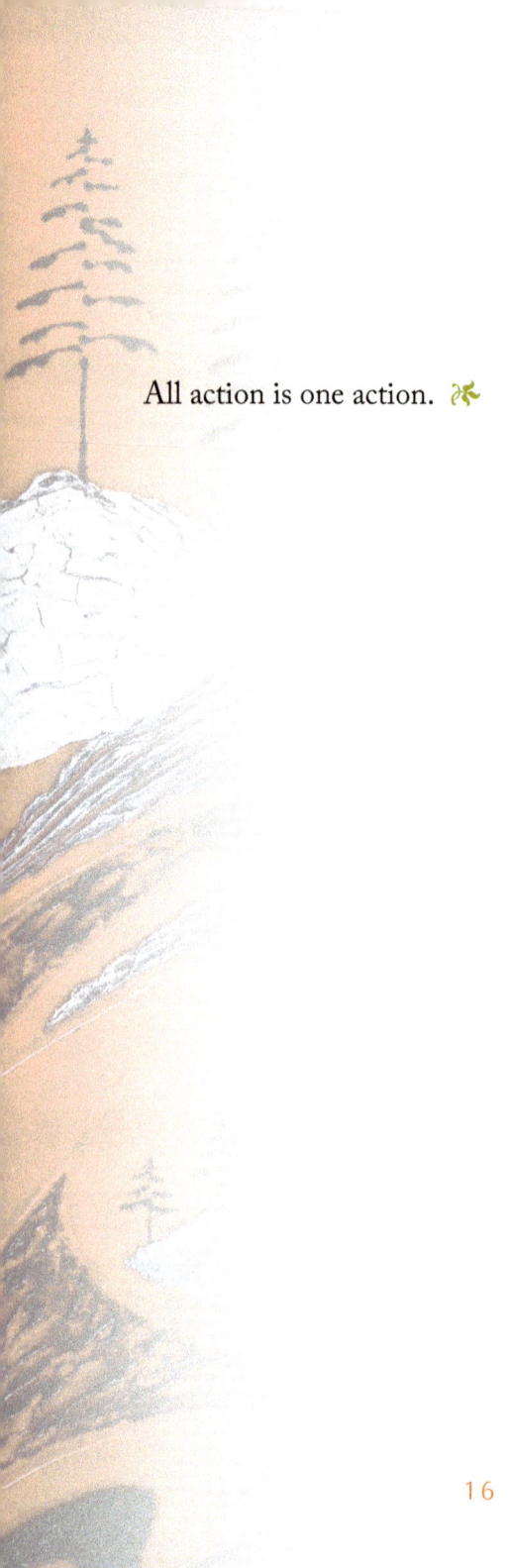

All action is one action.

There is only *One Indivisible Whole*.
All emanates from *This*.
The 'waving' of the ocean or the waving of your hand,
No difference.

POWER OF THE LAND

Beyond all names and forms,
Thoughts and musings,
Concepts and ideas,
It alone Is.

You are like space moving through space. *Formless.*
You cast no shadow,
You leave no footprints.

Reality is *dimensionless*.

There is nothing you need to *do* to become whole. Just simply *Be*. You are already complete.

Do not seek en[lighten]ment with a heavy heart.

Why are you still standing on the threshold knocking at the door?
Open the door and welcome your *Self* back to the home you never left! 🌱

Don't just wade in the water. You must dive into this *river* completely naked — stripped of all concepts, beliefs, and ideas.

And *swim* deeper and deeper to plumb the depths of this Unconditional Love.

REVERANCE

You are a manifestation of the One Universal Mind.
A single focal point of Consciousness expressing itself
through you and *as* you.

Does that not blow your mind?
No mind, no problem!

Silence is the greatest orator because it is the language of the *Self*. Why be so eager to speak when simply *being* is so effortless. The trees and flowers need no words for us to be astonished.

It has been ascribed many names: *Consciousness*, *Pure Awareness*, *the Absolute*. Such concessions must be made for the purpose of discourse.

Yet, *It* is *unnameable*.
Unutterable. ✺

There is absolutely nothing to be gained by the "person" from any non-dual teaching. In fact, the *pointings* function to orient you toward the complete annihilation of all sense of personhood.

Yet here you are with book in hand…

This is *fierce grace* in action!

As the identification with personhood dissolves, the entire world naturally dissolves along with it. The belief in a consensus reality that suggests we live in a world of solid objects no longer holds up. It is recognized as having been only a dream.

Everything is revealed as *Nothing*.

When the dreamer wakes up, does the dream not vanish too?

Paradoxically, it is through the dissolution of the self—and the concomitant experience of loss that follows—that one attains fulfillment beyond all imaginings.

You need not become an ascetic — there is nothing to renounce. Nothing to claim.

FALLING INTO LIGHTNESS

There is simply nothing, yet *It* encompasses everything. *It* is emptiness and fullness simultaneously.

When you see beyond all concepts of subject and object, it is obvious that you can neither possess nor renounce anything.

There is nothing to be gained,
nothing to be lost.

You are already *Everything* and *Nothing*.

Immaculate.

When walking through a forest amongst the trees, the rocks, and the rivers, the Sage clearly recognizes that there is absolutely nothing there – no trees, rocks, or river – yet walks blissfully along the path. Unperturbed.

In the *Seeing*, it is recognized that the Path never existed.

The experience of seeing a panoramic view of discrete objects is illusory. Everything is merely an appearance in Consciousness – the *real* allowing the *unreal* to appear.

Nothing appearing as *something*. ༜

The sound of water dripping off
the paddle,
The feeling of the wind as the
vessel glides,
The sight of the passing shoreline,
Of sun and clouds and sky.

Nature in all its uncompromis-
ing splendor,
Unfolding so beautifully before us,
Offering glimpses of what truly *Is*,
In a silent benediction.

In such perfect rhythm,
Stillness and movement
are indistinguishable.

In this *Oneness*,
All is revealed.

NORTHERN MUSE

Truth cannot be expressed in words or grasped by the intellect. If you want to know *Truth*, go and sit by a river in the forest and keep quiet.

You will find yourself amongst the most venerable of *Teachers*. 🌿

The lands and waters hold many truths for those who enter their wild and sacred spaces. We are the *One, Indivisible Whole* appearing as the many.

Everything that arises encompasses the *totality of all of existence*.

Everywhere you look,
there *You* are.

Are you ready to remember that *you* are…
every blade of grass?
Every insect.
Every bird.
Every tree.
Every drop of water.
Every grain of sand.
Every star.
Every galaxy…

When the beauty of the moonlight reflecting upon the water becalms us, something stirs within. And we begin to sense that we are *one* with the *Mystery* of everything that surrounds us — that we are no more separate from *the whole* than a wave is separate from the ocean.

You must dare to venture beyond all long-held ideas, concepts, and beliefs about *who* you are, if you are to discover *what you Are absolutely.*

It is closer than you think.
More intimate than thought.
Closer than anything you
can imagine.
So close you can never be separate
from *It*.
Closer than your own skin.
Closer than the breeze on your face.

You already know *It*.
You *are It*.
You have never been anything other
than *It*.
You have simply forgotten.

Remember This!

CALM OF THE WILD

To realize the Self,
Just keep quiet.
Entertain no thought.
Make no effort.
Closer than close,
It alone Is.

For a while you may appear to be wandering around as if in a fugue, having forgotten what you truly *Are*. But just as the clouds have no influence over the sun's ability to shine, *ignorance* cannot eclipse the truth of what you *Are*. ☙

You are *all-pervading Consciousness. Omnipresent.*
But this Truth cannot be grasped by the mind, only *realized*.

No effort is needed.
Simply allow yourself to "fall back" into this *silent Seeing.*

You are simply *Beingness, Being.*

The Truth is revealed in the *ever-present silence*. Yet, the ego will try to convince you that there is some kind of action you must perform, or some circumstance that you must change before you can discover *It*. But this is simply a ruse.

This *silence* cannot be interrupted by the activity and noise of the world, or by the agitation of a disquieted mind. *Truth* can be found right here, right now. In this *momentless moment*.

Just Be…within this soundless sound.

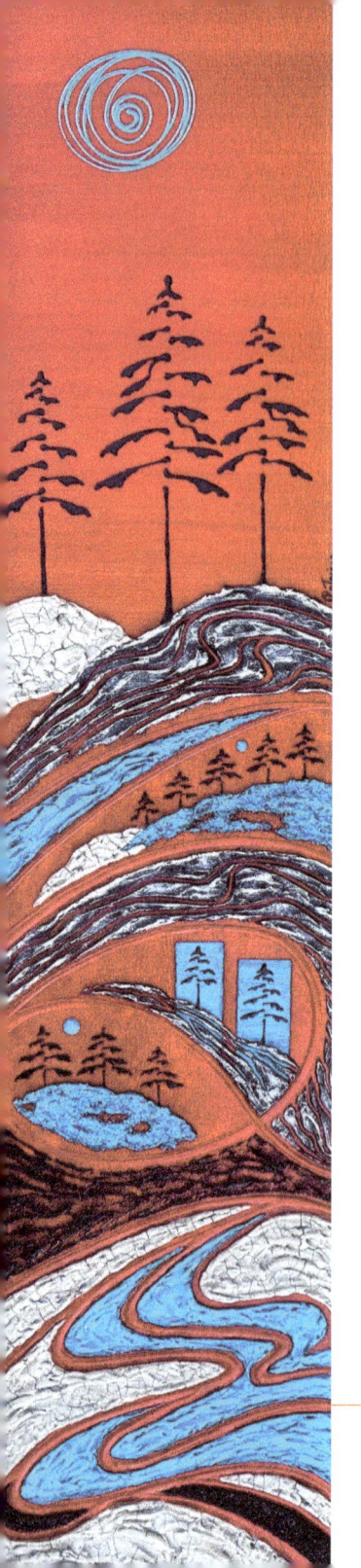

Do not confuse any kinds of spiritual experiences with Enlightenment, no matter how beguiling they
may appear.

At best, they are interesting.
At worst, a distraction. A hindrance.

They are not criteria upon which to base your "progress."
There is nothing beguiling or exotic about Enlightenment.

IF IT BE YOUR WILL

What gives rise to all changes but is itself *changeless*?

When there is a shift from the identity with personhood to the irrefutable recognition of one *Self* as *Pure Beingness*, the separate self is recognized as being only *apparently* real. Merely a thought believed in.

Outwardly, it may appear as if nothing has changed at all! "Your" life will seemingly go on as it always has. Relationships will still "happen," work will still get done, thoughts and feelings will still arise – but it is recognized that all of this happens for *no one*.

We can learn more about each other in the silence between us than in a thousand conversations.

Who is neither bound by time nor space?
Can this *One* be found?
Inquire within! 🌿

Through the dissolution of the sense of a separate self, the experience of being in a world that once appeared to be so frighteningly broken, is completely transformed.

When the veil of illusion drops, the *Unified Whole* is revealed.

Unutterable, It Is.

What you *truly are* is the most obvious of all, the simplest of all.
You are always looking at *It* and from *It*.
You are immersed in *It*.
You Are It!
And you have never been anything other than *It*.

But this expression of *Truth* is often met with a sense of bewilderment,
skepticism, and even suspect.
Yet, the confusion, doubt, and distrust, are also *It!*

You simply cannot be apart from *It*.
Can a flame can escape its own heat?

The deeper your experience of peace, the closer you may *feel* to *Self*. But you cannot get *closer* or *further* away.

There is *no distance.*

Just as the moon remains unfazed as its light dances upon the ripples of the ocean, *You* remain as the quintessential *abiding, unchanging, luminous Awareness*—untouched by the rising and falling of all apparent movement in the world.

MOON OVER WATER

There is no *single cause* of anything.

Absolutely everything that is happening is happening because of absolutely everything that is happening.

And there is absolutely nothing that is happening *absolutely*.

Everything that arises is the *whole* of everything.

It encompasses the totality of *All*. 🌿

Nothing lies outside of *This*.

There is no higher teaching than silence.

Like a shadow, everything that arises *is* and *is not*. ❧

No time.

No past,
No future,
No present.

No plans to make,
No path to follow.

No story.
Nothing to grasp onto,
Nothing to let go of.

Only Freedom Itself.

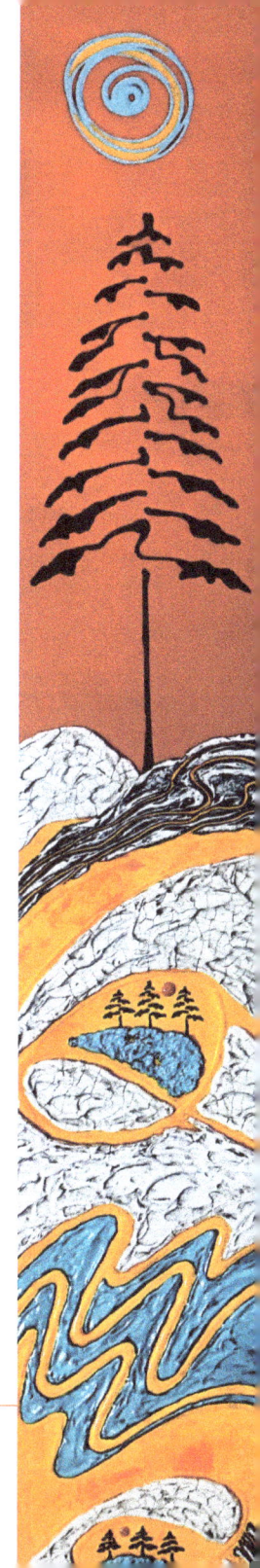

BE STILL MY HEART

We experience being in time and space when we perceive the world through a finite mind. But *This*, the Eternal reality of *spaceless space*, is not an experience. It is the *unchanging, distanceless infinitude*. ❧

Experiences by their very nature, come and go. But "This" is not an experience. What is it that lies beyond all notions of *coming* and *going*?

Nothing "happens,"
And *Nothing* "happens."
Contemplate this!

The past is both *real* and *unreal*, yet the mind cannot grasp this. And so, unable to see beyond mere appearances, it will argue vehemently that the past is unequivocally evidenced by one's memory of it.

But no moment is connected to any other moment. There is simply just *what Is*.

The realization that the past we "remember" never actually happened, makes absolutely no sense to the finite mind. Yet this is what is revealed in the Ultimate Seeing. *Irrefutably.*

We cannot expect the *finite* mind to grasp the vastness of the *Infinite*. 🌿

Time and space are mental constructs necessary for functioning in the *apparent* world. But they simply do not exist.

No *time*. No *space*. Just *This* 🌿

This is the only reality. ❧

This is *timeless*.

This is complete *emptiness*. *It* has absolutely no substance whatsoever.

The belief in the existence of free will is such a coveted one, that any suggestion to the contrary is profoundly threatening to the egoic mind; consequently, it will defend itself passionately against this limitation.

But the separate self is only *apparently* real. The person you imagine yourself to be is only a thought *believed in*. You are an *expression of Consciousness* — a part of the interconnectedness that makes up the fabric of the entire universe – not a *separate, independent entity*.

How could an individual have freedom of choice when ultimately, there is no individual?

When this is truly *Seen*, all arguments pertaining to the existence of free will simply collapse.

Absolutely everything that "happens" is intrinsically predeterminate in nature because everything that "happens," is a part of the totality of *all* apparent activity or functioning in the universe.

There is no separation. No "isolated" events. And so, it follows that even the thoughts that give rise to the *belief* in free will, must necessarily be a part of this predetermination.

It is only a *thought* that attributes the *freedom of choice* to the individual that we believe ourselves to be. But *Infinite Awareness* is all that exists. What we mistakenly claim as *my* freedom to make *my* choice, is made up of nothing other than Infinite Awareness acting according to its own nature.

BEING ALIVE TO MYSTERY

"This" is *Freedom*.
And everything arises from *This*.

You are an expression of the totality of all of existence.

But you cannot *imagine That!*

As we become increasingly self-aware, we begin to recognize and understand many of the ways that we have been conditioned throughout our lives – within our family systems, the cultures we were born into, the educational system, religious institutions, and all forms of media.

But as we become more adept at differentiating between the thoughts and belief systems that arise from our conditioning, and the deeper, more intuitive insights that feel more *spacious*, or even *inspired*, our lives can take on a depth and richness that appeared to be previously unavailable to us.

There is a tremendous freedom to be found in this process of maturation.

If we truly want to comfort and empower our children when they come to us with feelings of sadness, loneliness, fear, or self-doubt, we need to teach them ways to find peace and equanimity within the *silence* of their own *heart*. It is here that they will be reminded of their true beauty and innocence.

In this way, we can help to *illuminate* their way until they remember that *they are the source of the Light.*

Thoughts that arise from the conditioned, egoic mind are often fearful and accompanied by a feeling of *contraction*.

Thoughts arising from that which lies *beyond* the sense of personhood, feel peaceful and are accompanied by a feeling of *expansion*.

Our conditioning can lead us to feel compelled to ascribe meaning to events in our lives – whether they be splendorous, horrific, or somewhere in between.

But life simply happens. *No meaning, no purpose, no problem!*

When this is truly comprehended there can be a deep sense of relief. And it can allow us to *show up* and *be present* in a way that perhaps we never imagined possible; creating a profoundly enriched *lived experience* wherein we can partake in *everything* while holding on to *nothing*.

The one who truly grasps the deeper meaning of this understands it as the antithesis of nihilism: perhaps even its antidote.

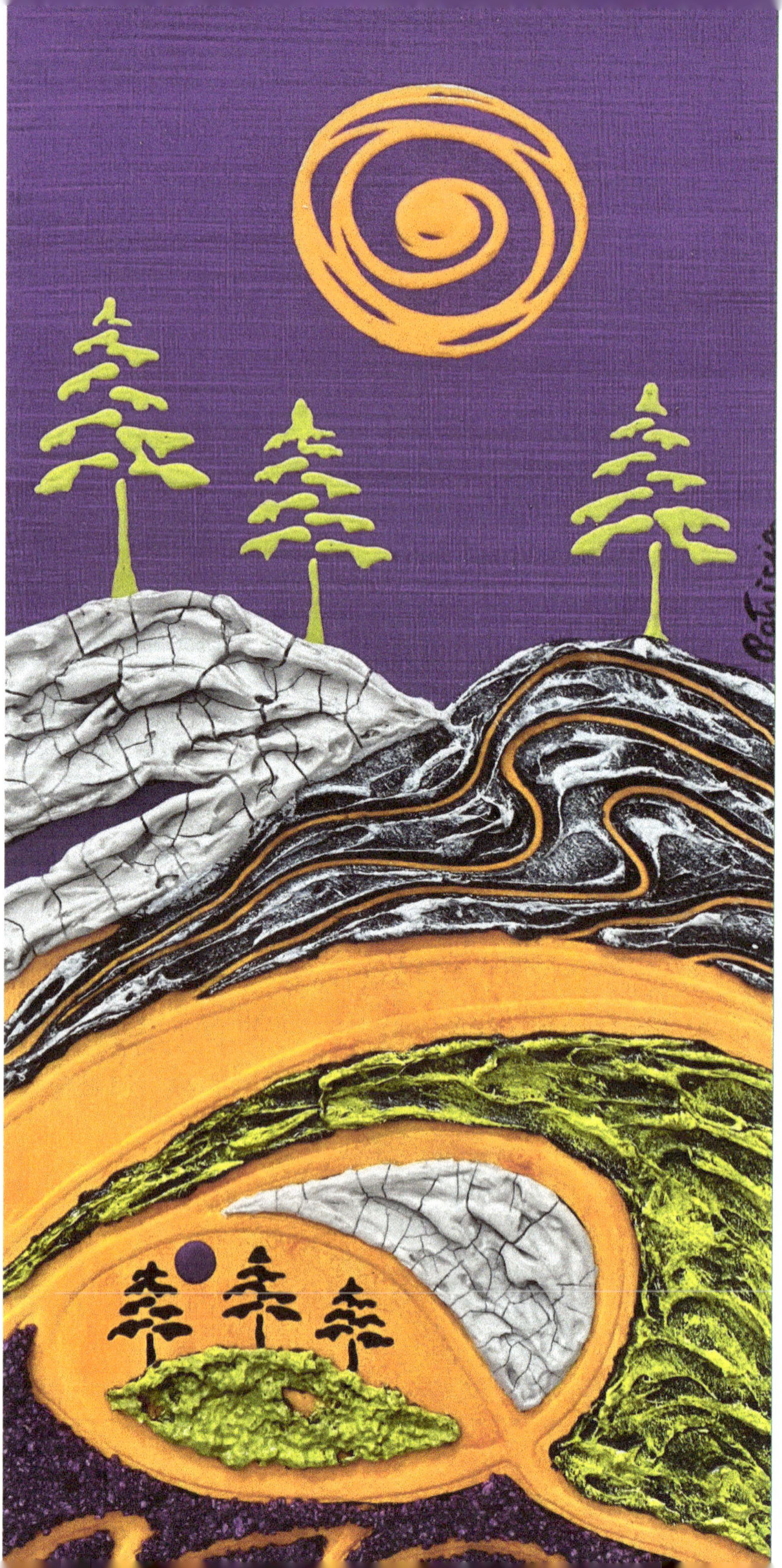

The very act of "making an effort" eclipses our *Seeing*. ❧

CHASING MY DREAMS

What appears to happen is the only thing that *can* appear to happen.

Everything is just *arising*. It is not arising *for* anyone.

There is no *thinker* of thoughts. The "thinker" itself is merely a thought.

Thoughts, emotions, and feelings "happen." For *no one* at all. ✿

There is just *Awareness*. There is no one *being* Aware.

There is just *doing*.
Just *hearing*.
Just *seeing*.
Just *thinking*.

Everything that is happening is just happening. There is nothing being *done by* or *happening to* anyone. 🌿

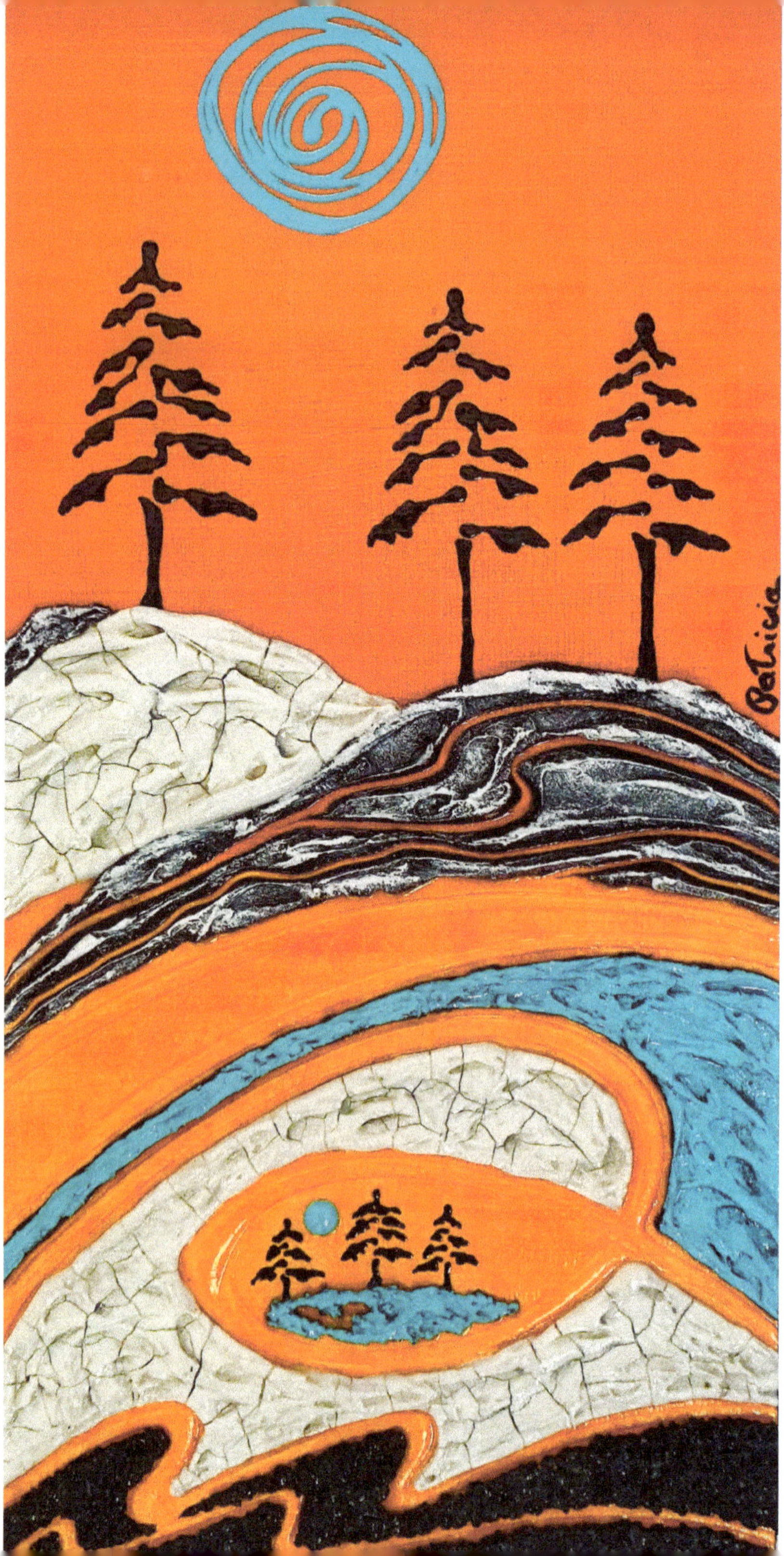
Patricia

Awakening is impersonal. There is no "person" that wakes up. One wakes up from the *dream of personhood* — from the idea of a separate "me."

A CHANCE ENCOUNTER ON THE WAY HOME

All seeking energy simply dissolves in the *Ultimate Seeing* — just like the mist on a river vanishes when it is touched by the radiance of the morning sun.

Looking for one *Self* is like a wave looking for the ocean. *It* is what you *Are*. ❦

The very act of seeking obscures the truth of what *You* are. To *seek* there must be two: the *seeker* and the *sought*.

How can we possibly go looking for *our own Self?* Know that there is only *One*.

Enlightenment is the *intuitive, direct recognition in the heart* that you are Pure Consciousness. Absolute Beingness.

It is your natural state of *Being*.
And the end of all seeking.

Your very pursuit of Enlightenment is your prison.

Abandon all efforts,
Forsake all intentions,
Let go of all beliefs — even the belief
in *Enlightenment*.
Hold onto nothing,
Not even these words.

And you will discover that you are *Freedom Itself*.

It is beyond all imaginings.
Beyond all understanding.

Truth is not an opinion.

WHEN NATURE SPEAKS

True surrender is not done *by* anyone or *for* anyone.

It is the *action* of *non-action*.

No *sadhana*, or spiritual practice, can lead you to *what Is* already.

All forms of practice imply that there is a path to take,
Somewhere else to be,
Distance to be travelled,
A chasm to be crossed,
But *It* is right here.

Why venture elsewhere to find what is already *here*?
What is *You*!

Awakening will *happen* when it *happens*. It needs no interference from you. No meditation, no prayer, no breathwork, no yoga.

Practice may happen or not happen.
Awakening may happen or not happen.

No causality or alliance exists between the two.

There can be a sense of bewilderment upon hearing that nothing can be done to either hasten or slow down *Self-realization*, yet that engaging in some kind of practice can affect your process.

Ah, the beauty of paradox!

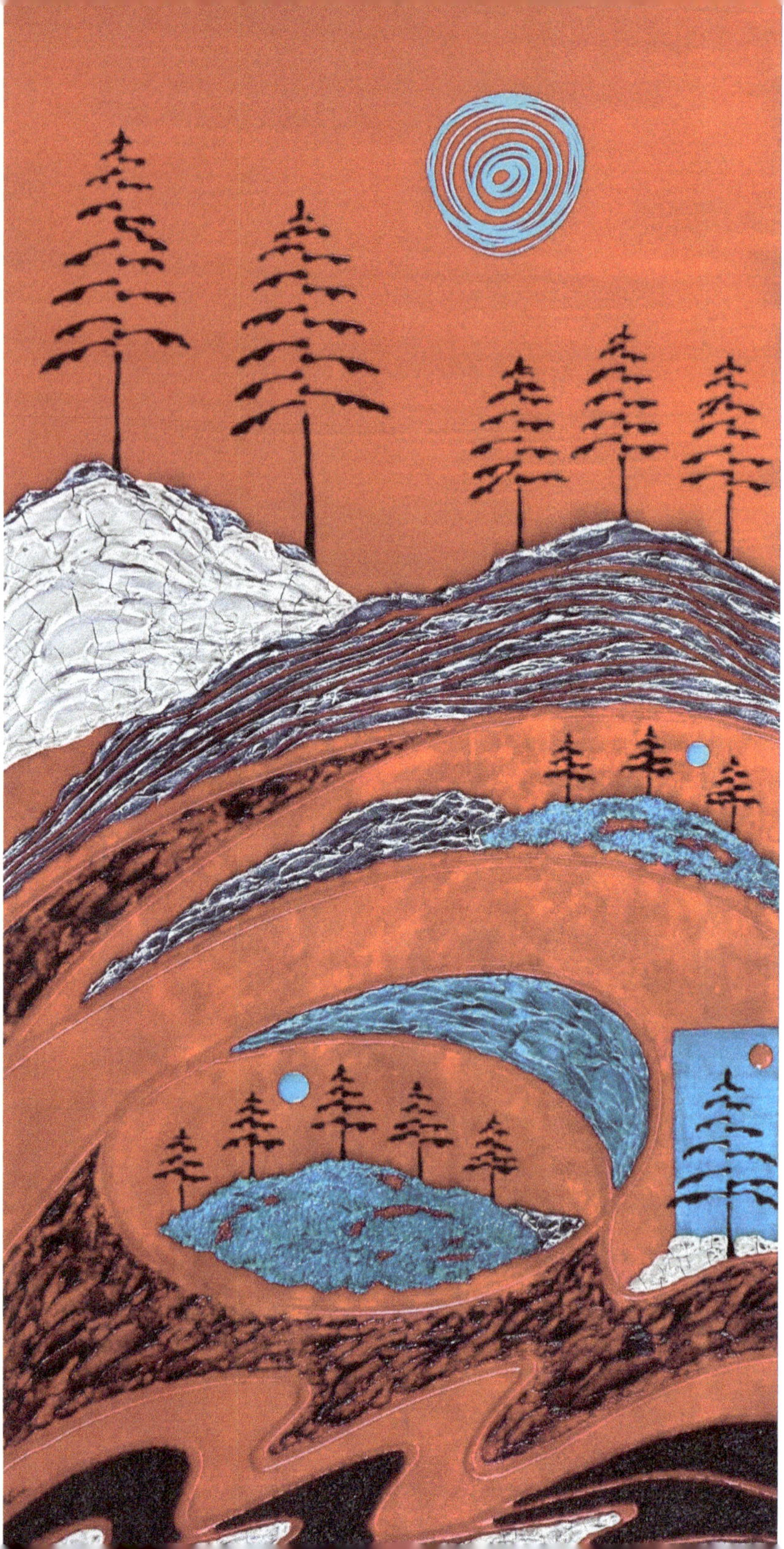

Liberation often "happens" when the futility of seeking is seen. When the fascination with your own narrative fizzles out and you are no longer beset with the need to know how *your story* ends! 🌿

LIGHT MY FIRE

The deeper the Truth, the greater the paradox.

The desire to meditate often falls away after *Liberation*—effortlessly and without any intention. It may simply be seen that there is no longer anyone *to* engage in any kind of practice, and the perceived need no longer arises.

Instead, you may often find yourself simply sitting in the *silence of Pure Awareness*. Within the tranquility of *empty, spaceless space*.

Pure Awareness is your *natural, effortless* state of being. When you find yourself *seeking* the Truth, you have simply forgotten what you are.

You are already that which you are seeking.
You have never been anything else.
You can never *be* anything else. 🌿

What the seeker is ultimately seeking is the end to their own *self*.
It takes courage to walk the *pathless path* that leads to nowhere at all!

Nothing can be gained. Nothing can be lost. There is simply, *Nothing*.

All manifestations are *Nothing* appearing as *something*.

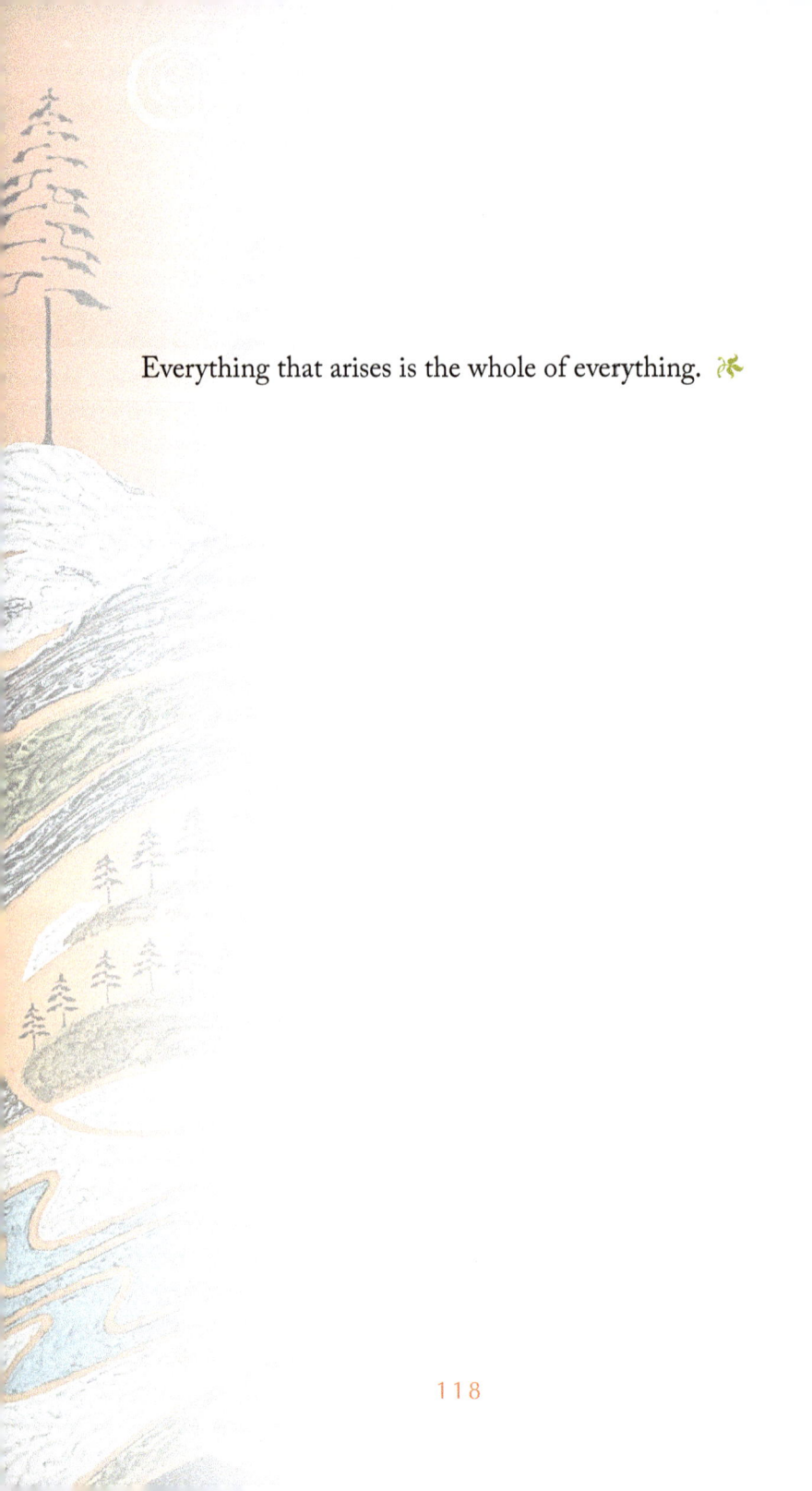

Everything that arises is the whole of everything.

Mind cannot help you here,
It is an obstacle on the "path"
to Awakening.
Forget everything you have learned,
Don't think.
Make no effort whatsoever.

Just dive right into your *heart space*.
Leave all you think you know behind,
And go deeper and deeper.

It is the portal to the entire
universe.

RAPTUROUS HEART

Time is an illusion.
The idea of a past cannot exist outside of memories,
The future, outside of imagination.
There isn't even a "now."

Ask yourself, "When does 'now' become the past?"
There is always *just This*.

Don't search for the *Truth* elsewhere.
It is right *here*.

To suggest that time is simply an illusion appears ludicrous to the mind.

Yet when the *Veil of Maya* drops, the illusion of time is seen through —
completely and irrevocably.

The illusion of movement within time is created by the ever-presence of *timeless* "*moments.*" There is no beginning or end to the rising or setting of the sun.

There is just *one timeless reality.*

The *totality of All* is revealed within the realm of the *Eternal,* beyond all concepts of time.

The *Ultimate Seeing* is irrefutable,
Beyond all imaginings.
Indescribable. ༄

It is our minds that create the
illusion of time.

Memories of past experiences
creating nostalgia and regrets,
Thoughts about the future
spawning our hopes and fears,
Beliefs about events that
appear to be happening in the
present moment.

Yet it is all imagined! We are
the main character in our own
Divine play!
There is no past,
No future,
Not even a "now."

There is just what *appears* to
be happening,
Just what is arising.

Upon Awakening this is known beyond all concepts of *knowing* and *not knowing*.

SEEING BEYOND THE ILLUSION

Only the *timeless* exists.

The whole idea of *time* is simply a thought,
It exists in the mind alone.
Our memories create a belief in "a time before," and lead us to deduce there will be "a time in the future."

We habitually base our whole worldview on a fallible mental construct!

You are not your mind.
Know this and *be still*.

All our experiences come and go.
What is it that does *not* come and go?

Only the *changeless* is real,
All else is illusion.

We have been conditioned to believe in the concept of *cause and effect* — in a relationship between two separate events that *appear* to "happen." But the belief in one event preceding and causing another to occur, appears to be true only when observed through the limited perspective of the finite mind.

There is no "before," no "after."
There is only what is arising.

Every *momentless moment* contains the totality of the entire universe.

In the *Seeing*, time and space are revealed as completely illusory, rendering all queries relating to *cause and effect* meaningless.

There is only *One*.
Only *Brahman*.

BOUNDLESS LIGHT

Absolutely everything is as it is because the whole universe is as it is.
Uncaused.

No time.
No space.

Only that which lies beyond all concepts of time and space exists.
The Eternally present, dimensionless "here."

Whatever is happening is the totality of all of existence. ❧

Time and space are simply *This*, appearing as the experience of *time and space*.

Everything is just "This," appearing as *something*. 🌿

This moment is not connected to any other moment.
You have never *done* anything.
Or *been* anyone.
You are not a person *living* a life.
You *ARE* life!

RUGGED BEAUTY

No *'you,'* no karma. End of *story*!

Imagine the kind of world we would live in if more human beings understood *everything* as the manifestation of the *One, Indivisible Whole* — and their way of being in the world was a reflection of that understanding.

If the Absolute was known to be implicit in all things *animate* and *inanimate*.

In the *Seeing*, the once deeply entrenched identification with being the "doer" of actions, simply and effortlessly dissolves. It is recognized beyond all doubt that *you* have never *done* anything in your entire life.

You discover that "you" were only a thought. That you never actually existed. *Ever.*

Within this understanding comes the realization that there is nothing you must do. Nothing you *can* do.

Meanwhile, everyone is running about trying to figure out *what* they are supposed to do and *when* they are supposed to do it. It is completely preposterous! Yet here we are!

There is only what *appears* to be "happening."
Everything simply arises,
For no reason.

Whatever is "happening" is the only thing that *can* be "happening."

The person we believe ourselves to be is simply an *activity* of Consciousness arising *within* Consciousness. A mere "countenance" on the face of Consciousness, not a distinct, separate entity.

Thoughts appear to arise, and activity appears to take place, but there is no independent *thinker* of thoughts or *doer* of actions.

All that exists is the *One Infinite Consciousness*.
And *You Are That*.

Refuse to stay *asleep*. You were *born* to remember. 🌱

ON A MARVELOUS NIGHT

In the *final Seeing*, everything must go. *Everything!*

Even the *illusion* is an illusion. There is only *This*.

No one can *attain* Liberation.

Liberation happens *from* the person, not *to* the person.

There is no one *to* Liberate!

You talk, yet there is *no one* speaking,
You hear, yet there is *no one* listening,
You see, yet there is *no one* seeing.

There is simply *no one*.

There is nowhere to go,
Nothing to do.

Just keep quiet.
When "noise" arises, gently come back to the *Silence*,
and rest in the *ever-present Stillness*.

Be steadfast.
Your efforts will be rewarded.

It is your destiny to wake up to what truly *Is*. To what you truly *Are*.

It is simplest of *ALL*. The purest of *ALL*. The most obvious of *ALL*. *It* is quite simply, *ALL*.

MORNING SONG

Even the thought "this is not *It*," is It.
There's just no getting away from It!

There is no identification *here*,
No reference points.
No inside or outside,
Above or below,
Right action or wrong action.
No "you."
Just pure *Isness*.

There is nothing here for "you."
Nothing here for the person you believe yourself to be.
Are you ready to stand without any concepts or mental structures to hold you up?
To release all identification, labels, and ideas about *who* and *what* you are?
To be stripped *naked*.

Are *you* ready to "die"?
It is not for the faint of heart!

To find out what you *are*, you must find out what you are *not*.

Neti neti. Neither this nor that.

In the end, even the negator must be negated.

In the light of pure *Seeing*, you discover that you are nothing but vast emptiness. Yet the entire universe is contained within *You*.

All thoughts, feelings, perceptions, and sensations are simply phenomenal aspects of the human experience—arising within consciousness from *Nothingness* and dissolving back into *Nothingness*.

They belong to *no one*. ❧

You merely think yourself into a perceived existence whenever you believe that you are a person. But you are the *non-phenomenal, non-conceptual, shapeless Awareness*. Beyond all concepts of *being* and *non-being*.

Conditioning has you believing that you wake up in the morning and begin each day anew. *But do you?* And is it *really* a new day?

Waking up in the morning simply "happens." For *no one.* Yet by virtue of the memories of what you believe is "your" life, you resurrect the apparent "story of you," again and again…

But this story is simply an *idea*. A *thought* super-imposed over the reality of what truly *Is*.

Observe this! It just might be *the end of you!*

A NEW DAY

You are the ever-present background of all experience from which all thoughts and beliefs about personhood arise.

In the quest for the Truth, nondual *pointings* function as a compass of sorts, constantly orienting you back toward your own *Self*.

Every belief you hold about *who* and *what* you are must fall away.

No thought of "you" can bear the radiance of your own *Being*. ❧

Mind creates the experience of duality — of subject and object. The *seer* and the *seen*. But upon further inquiry we discover there is no one *doing* the looking.

There is no one *being* aware.
There is only *Awareness*.

Only *Awareness* can be aware of *Itself*.

But what is *prior to*, even *subtler* than Awareness?

Only the *Absolute* exists *absolutely*.

There is a natural *stillness* that exists. An ever-present *silence*.
So vast and spacious that there is nowhere where it is *not* — and yet it is nowhere at all.

It is the essence of your own *Being*.

Look! ⁓

NORTHERN BEAUTY

Silence simply *Is*.
Eternal, luminous, impeccable.

Every face is your face.
Every joy, every sorrow, is *Yours* alone.
How could one not fall silent in the immensity of this *Seeing*?

Justification keeps us in bondage.

Seeking is simply *It* experienced as seeking.

You cannot find what you are seeking by looking for it elsewhere.
Stay right where you are.
It is where you are looking *from*.

What lies just *behind* your experience of seeing? Simply shifting your attention away from whatever you are *looking at* and putting it onto the *experience of looking*, creates a "space" in which all identification with the person that you have been conditioned to believe that you are, can drop away so that you might recognize *what* you are *absolutely*.

Just sit in silence.
Make no effort whatsoever.
Don't think about anything.
Not even Enlightenment.
Let the silence devour who you believe yourself to be
and replace you, with *You*.

Don't flinch when your head is inside the lion's
mouth.

In the end, even the seeker disappears in the *Seeing*. 🌿

WALKING EACH
OTHER HOME

There never was a *seeker* to *seek*. ❧

It can only be realized in the cessation of seeking. The very act of seeking implies two — reinforcing the belief in a *seeker* and that which is being *sought*.

There is only *One*.

There is *just This. Just This.*

That which is *real* appears to veil itself when we have a preoccupation with worldly activities and events.

But no true or lasting satisfaction can be found outside of *It*. ❧

We cannot find Truth in the objects of our experience because there simply are no discreet objects. Everything that we perceive to be real in the external world is merely a manifestation of the *One, Indivisible Whole* appearing as the many.

Instead, simply turn your attention inward.
Abandon all intentions,
Relinquish all expectations.

Cease all striving to *achieve* anything.
There is absolutely nothing you need to *do*.
Just keep quiet.

The Truth is "hiding" in plain sight.

If you are tired of searching why not simply stop?
Don't follow a single thought.
Just allow your mind to be still.
Make no effort whatsoever.

There is no need for your imagination here. Let go of your fascination with all activity – both worldly and spiritual. *Don't touch anything.*

This alone will create the space for the most astonishing discovery.
By simply doing *nothing* you gain *everything*!

There is no doer of actions.
No thinker of thoughts.

There is nothing that can be *attained*. Only *realized*.

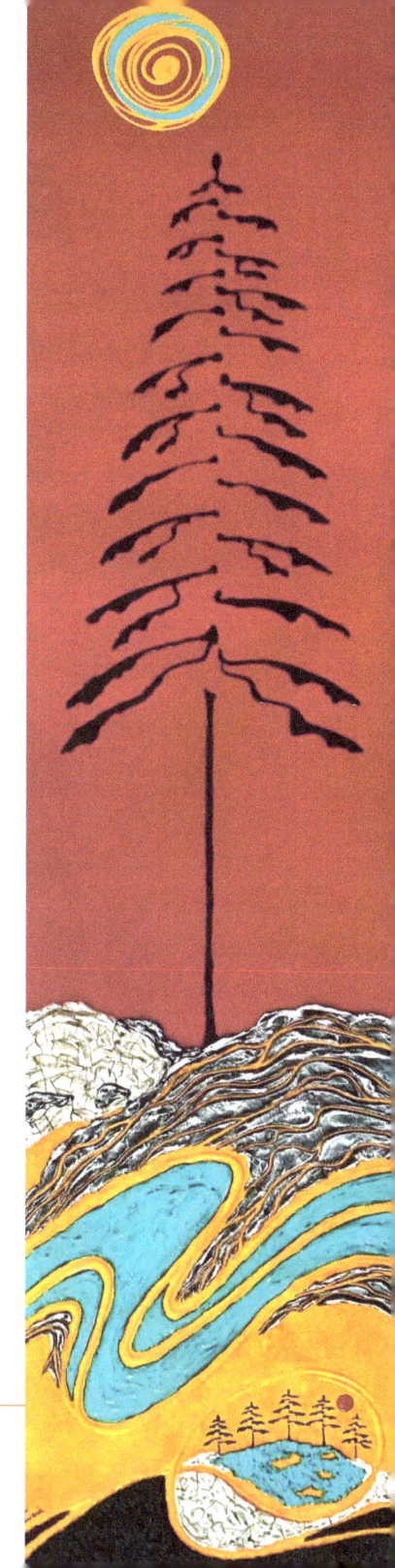

WAITING FOR THE DAWN

What exists in the space *before* your thoughts?

What is *ever-present* in the background of all experience?

The ego is simply a *movement* within the all-pervasive, infinite field of Consciousness. Still, we are lulled into believing that this infinitesimal, limited aspect of ourselves is who we *are*.

But this is merely a concept *believed in*.
It has no substance or reality whatsoever.

So much attention can be directed toward the objective content of experience that we can easily overlook what is *silent* and *ever-present*.

Don't give your power away to the incessant workings of your mind.
When you really investigate your thoughts, you will find that they consist of nothing at all.

Why allow yourself to be troubled by *nothing*?!

The recognition of our true nature as *boundless, formless Awareness* is not an "experience." Experiences, such as thoughts, feelings, and perceptions, by their very nature, *come* and *go*. Find that which does not come and go.

Within benevolence
and barbarity,
Joy and pain,
Love and contempt,
Light and darkness,
Honour and shame,
Grace and disgrace,
It alone Is.

STILLNESS IN MOTION

Self-realization is nothing extraordinary. In fact, it is "extra"-ordinary. So *familiar*, so *natural*. So *simple*, that for a time this *Seeing* can easily go unnoticed by the mind.

It is your conditioning that has led you to believe that you are a person *living* a life, but the person you believe yourself to be does not exist. That 'one' has never existed.

You are the *vast, timeless, immutable, boundless One,* in which all apparent manifestations appear and disappear. Including the manifestation of the idea of "you"!

The recognition of what you truly are beyond name and form must be apperceived.
It cannot be revealed to you by *anyone* or *anything* outside of your own
Self.

Know that the Truth is being revealed unceasingly inside the quietness of your own heart.

This is Grace.
Just *be still* and *listen.*

We imagine that we are a *doer* doing — and we even make conjectures about what other people are doing and not doing!

There is no one doing anything.

We are obsessing over ghosts!

Believing that you are the *doer* of actions is like the trembling aspen believing that it flutters its own leaves.

Whatever you can perceive cannot be *what you are*. *You* are *That* which exists prior to all phenomena that arise and are perceived.

The activity and "noise" of the world cannot disturb *You*.
You are the *Silence* from which all apparent manifestations arise and that which they dissolve back into.

You remain as *formless Awareness*.
Untroubled. 🌿

JIIGIBIIG ("ALONG THE SHORE"
IN ANISHINAABEMOWIN)

Where are you trying to go?
And why so hurriedly?
Don't you know that *You* are already *everywhere!*
And *nowhere!*

There is no distance to travel.
No time.
Nothing to figure out.

Just be still and be *Home.*

There is no effort needed to *Be*.
Nothing that needs to be done,
Nowhere to go.

There is simply *gorgeous, effortless, stillness!*

Sat. Chit. Ananda.
Beingness. Consciousness. Bliss.

One indivisible Trinity.

Relinquish all sense of doing,
Abandon all thoughts,
Give up all speech,
And find your *Self* here.

Grasp at nothing,
Turn all your attention inward.
Keep quiet,
And abide in the *Self* alone.

There is nothing that needs to be done,
No distance to be travelled,
Nothing to believe,
Nothing to declare,
For you to recognize who *You* are *already!*

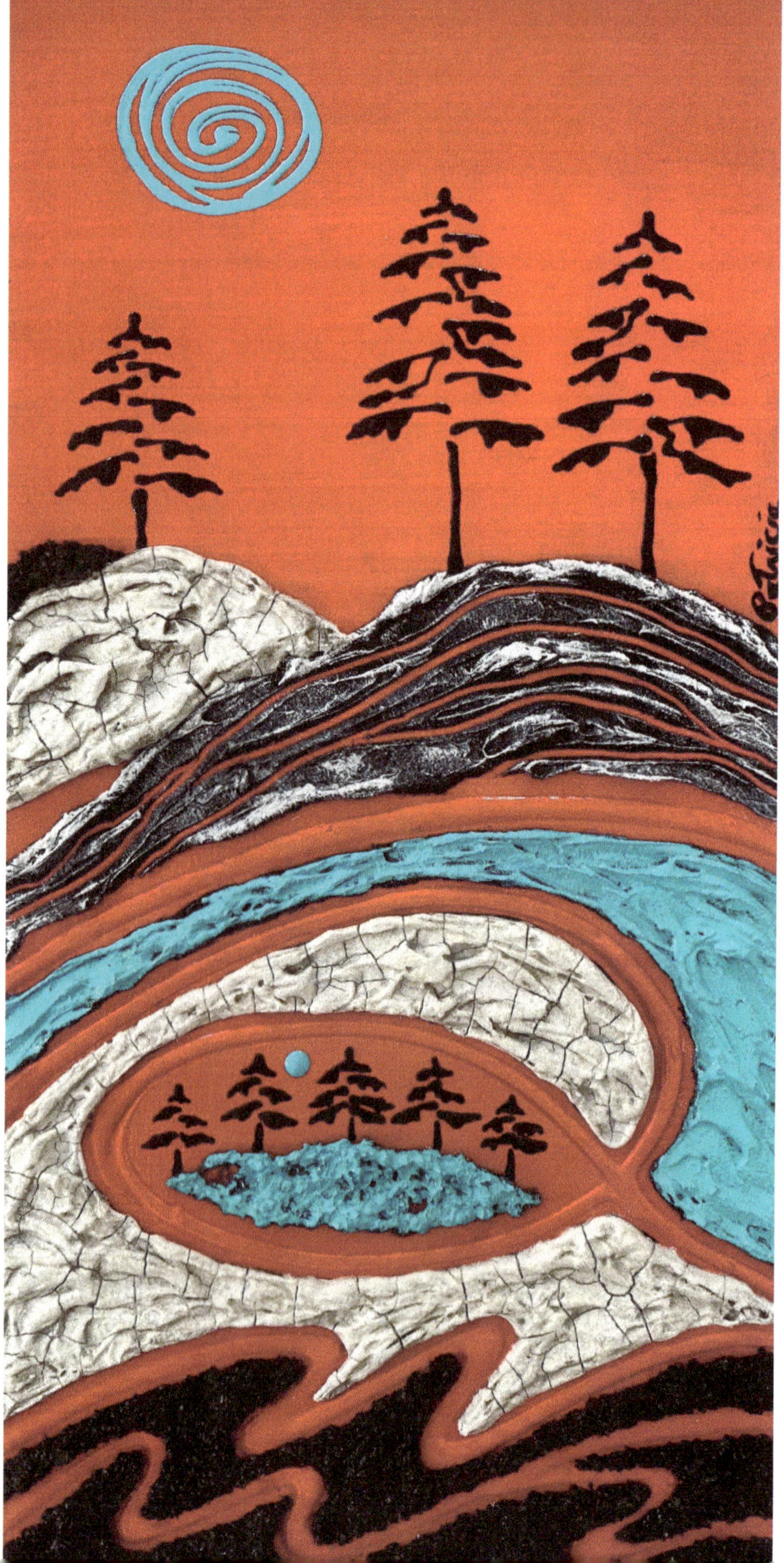

There is simply pure *Nothingness* appearing as everything.

Mysterious, unknowable, ineffable Nothingness!

SIMPLY DELIGHTFUL

The fullness of *This* is beyond all description. How could anyone describe
such an unfathomable Love?

This can only be seen through the *eyes of the Heart*. ༉

Tat tvam asi. You Are That.

This cannot be grasped by the mind. Beyond all categories of thought, *It* transcends everything that the "person" can *imagine*.

In this *Seeing*, absolutely nothing changes yet absolutely everything is transformed. 🌿

The one identified with personhood remains restless even while appearing peaceful.

The one established in the *Self* remains peaceful even while appearing restless. ❧

When it is clearly recognized that there is *no person*, the stories we once held onto about our "past," what is happening "now," what we imagine might happen in the "future," are recognized as having no inherent reality. No substance whatsoever.

And they are no longer energized through our attention.

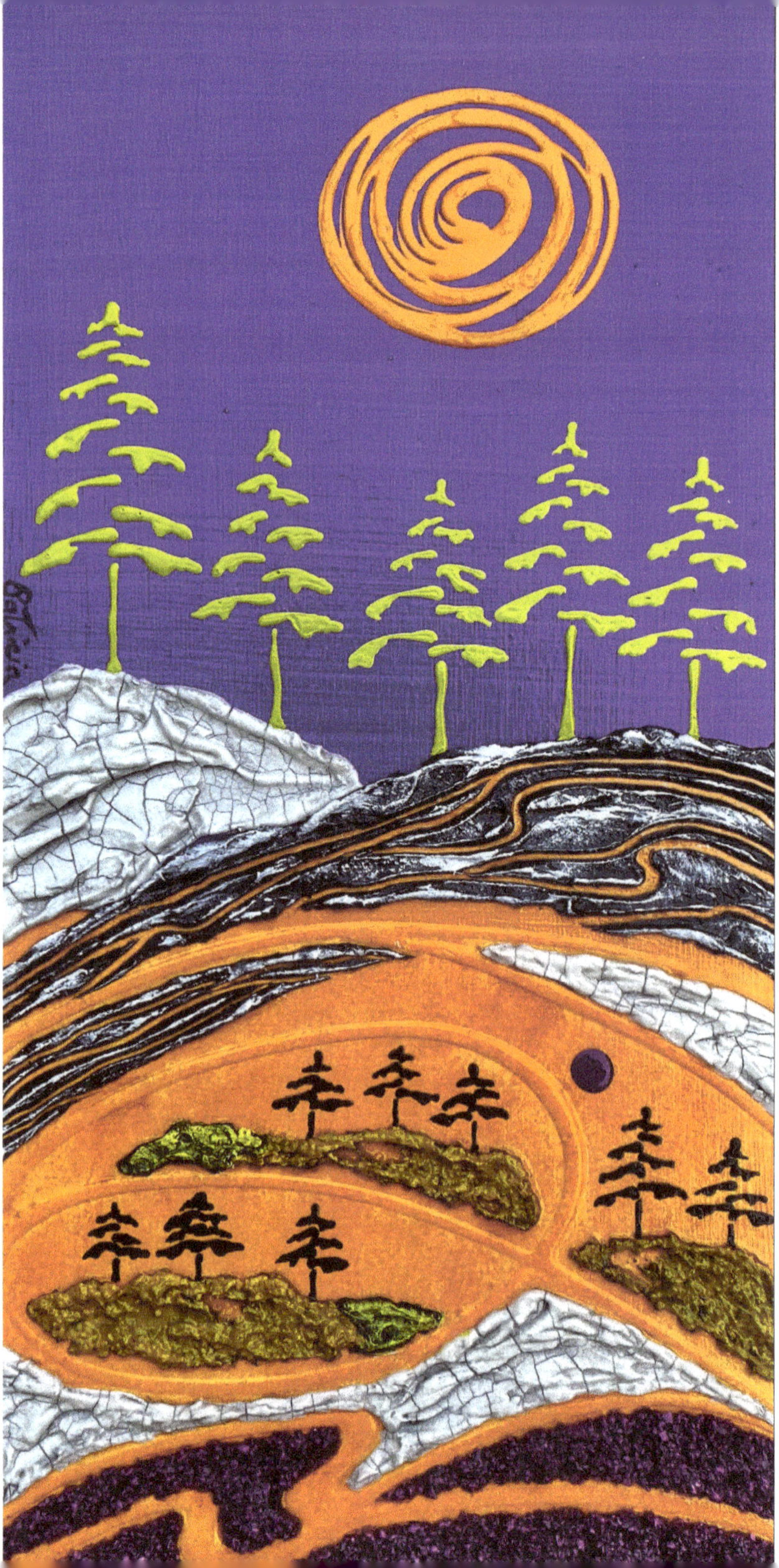

The *final Seeing* does not diminish or deny the human experience.
However, the emotional entanglement that is fundamental to the "story of *me*," simply dissolves.

There is a profound freedom in this recognition.

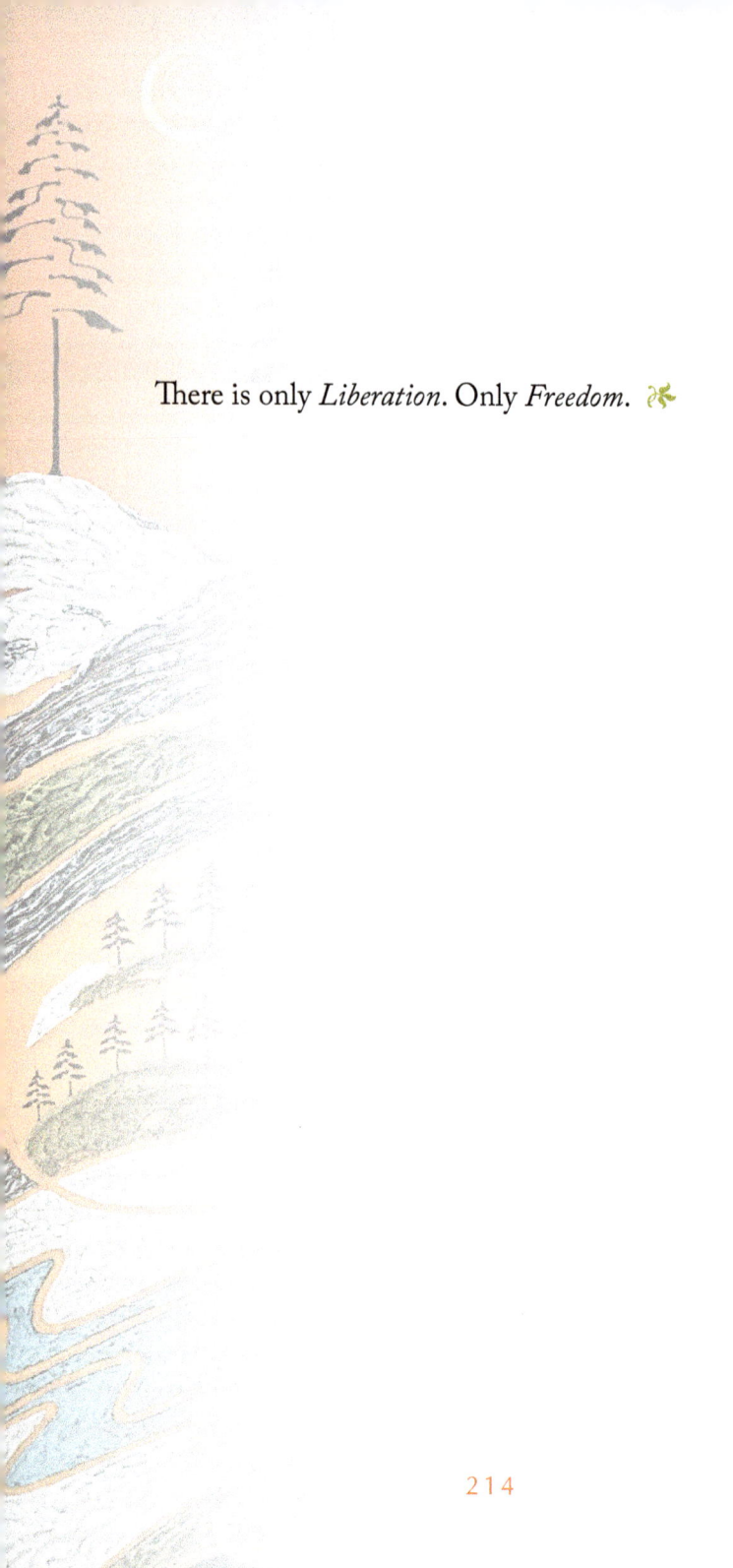

There is only *Liberation*. Only *Freedom*.

There is nothing to *do*. Nowhere to *go*. Nothing to *become*.

Only *This* IS.

No matter how *broken* you may feel, you are *Whole*,
No matter how *depraved* you may feel, you are *Pure*,
No matter how *disconnected* you may feel, you are *Oneness*,
No matter how *enslaved* you may feel, you are *Freedom*,
No matter how *entitled* you may feel, you are *Nothing*,
No matter how *worthless* you may feel, you are *Everything*.

There is only *One*.
Yet I lie beyond all ideas of Unity and duality.

Beyond all notions of desireless and desire,
Stillness and movement,
Freedom or bondage,
Fulfillment and seeking,
The changeless and changeful,
Purity or impurity,
Formlessness and form.

I am boundless.
Residing in the *Heart*,
I AM and I AM NOT.

All dissolves in this *Seeing*.

Nothing survives the *Truth*.

Why be so timid?
Why not recognize your own True Nature as *Brahman?*

You are the embodiment of Absolute Reality.
Ultimate Freedom,
Pure, effortless, choiceless Awareness,
All-pervading Consciousness.

There is nothing *other* than what you Are.
Recognize this!

Awaken and be joy-filled.

These words were written by *no one*, for *no one*.

A WALK ON THE WILD SIDE III

ISNESS

PATRICIA GRAY

Where is existence or non-existence?
Where is Unity or duality?
Nothing emanates from me.
No more can be said.[1]

Ashtavakra Gita [20:14]

---

1 Marshall, B. (Trans.). *Ashtavakra Gita, Chapter 20, Verse 14*. (n.d.). Ashtavakra Gita, Realface Press, 2023.

ISNESS

MOOSE RIVER,
JAMES BAY LOWLANDS
PHOTO COURTESY OF DONNA GLENESK

PATRICIA GRAY

The End
(of absolutely Nothing!)